Postcards from Cramlington

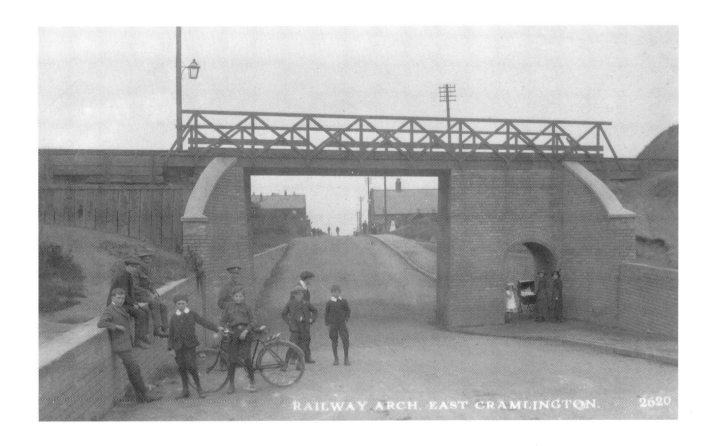

RAILWAY ARCH, EAST CRAMLINGTON. 2620

by Brian Godfrey

Sea View Villas, Cramlington. A postcard by Robert Johnston & Sons of Gateshead in his 'Monarch Series'. Johnston was a frequent visitor to Cramlington and a number of his postcards appear in this book.

Previous page: The railway arch at East Cramlington – another Monarch Series postcard.

Also available from Summerhill Books

Cramlington Parkside School Remembered

Wartime Memories – Stories of the Second World War in the North East

Deaths, Disasters & Dastardly Deeds in the North East

visit our website to view our full range of books: **www.summerhillbooks.co.uk**

Copyright Brian Godfrey 2013

First published in 2013
Reprinted in 2014 by

Summerhill Books
PO Box 1210, Newcastle-upon-Tyne NE99 4AH

www.summerhillbooks.co.uk

email: summerhillbooks@yahoo.co.uk

ISBN: 978-1-906721-73-2

Introduction

The title of this book is *Postcards from Cramlington*, however, I have also used cards depicting other places as additional illustrations and to gain a better understanding of the wider social implications of events.

The 'Golden Age' of postcard sending and postcard collecting is generally recognised as being the ten or so years before the First World War. The popularity for postcards as a means of relatively fast and cheap communication was never equalled again outside of this period. Many cards can be found with the simple message 'For your collection'. Albums of the time contain a diverse mixture of subjects as just about every subject that the mind can conjure was offered for sale by publishers.

The postcard at that time became the Edwardian equivalent of our text message. The Post Office could provide three deliveries daily and very often would deliver on the day of posting, depending upon distance. Unfortunately the unpleasantness between England and Germany in 1914, put a bit of a dampener on this idyllic situation. For reasons of cost and superior printing techniques most cards of the period were printed in Germany, published and sold by outlets in England. Cramlington had its own publisher in Robson Brothers of Cramlington Post Office, the hairdressers next to the Church in Village Square was once their premises. Anyway, it would not do for Britain to have any 'truck' with the 'Hun' so the trade was stopped. We spent the war years issuing mainly patriotic subjects, warships, aircraft, Zeppelins etc and those that appealed directly to the

A Cramlington postmark from a card featured in this book.

heart with flowers and angels and babies and poetry. All very boring no doubt but thanks must go to those photographers who roamed the countryside with their cumbersome equipment producing real photographic cards of people, places and incidents that fascinate the collector today.

Distinction must be made here between the one who collects cards for their aesthetic beauty and he who collects cards that show places and people as they were. I am of the latter persuasion but consider that while the image depicted is important the message it bears is unique and worthy in some cases of mention. This is especially so with cards sent during the Great War. The message can give an insight into the lives of the senders and recipients, holidays, entertainment, relationships and serving soldiers to their loved ones telling of guard duty, drills, hopes and fears are the handwritten thoughts of those long gone.

Station Road, Cramlington.

A splendid card, originally colour, by Robson Brothers, Cramlington posted to Tarset in 1925.

For my father
Bill Godfrey
of Nelson Village

Village Road, Cramlington.

Acknowledgements

I would like to thank the following people who have helped with the publication of this book:

Anthony Smithson of Keel Row Books, North Shields, Geoffrey Berriman, Tom Hutchinson, Robert Mitchelson, George Nairn and Sharyn Taylor for typing the manuscript,

Bibliography

Cramlington District Co-operative Society Ltd Jubilee Souvenir, 1881-1911
Longbenton and District Council Guide
Homing Pigeon Annual, 1917
Regimental Histories of the 16th & 18th Northumberland Fusiliers
Biggles and the Black Peril by Captain W.E. Johns

Postcards From Cramlington

This card was posted from Cramlington on 27th October 1903 and is addressed to 'Miss Huntley, High Street, Amble'. The image, however, appears to be somewhat earlier than this date and shows the Church and Village Square, circa 1895-1900. The row of cottages adjoining the Fox & Hounds Hotel, were removed shortly after in favour of the present buildings. The cottage gardens are railed off

Cramlington Church.

and appear to be well tended, with shrubs, flowers and vegetables showing. Cottagers stand in front of their doors looking towards the camera with curiosity – probably a highlight in an otherwise ordinary day. A horse and cart stands outside the Fox & Hounds Hotel, no prizes for guessing where the driver might be! My mother's uncle, Mr Richard Nevins, was a publican at the Fox & Hounds Hotel for a number of years in the 1920s, before moving to the Boundary Inn at East Cramlington. My mother and grandmother stayed with 'Uncle Dick' at Cramlington before moving to Fencehouses, County Durham to live with an aunt. The road appears to be unmetalled and must have been a muddy nightmare during the winter months.

The message on the card reads: 'Play up Amble you lucky lads, Dudley will defeat you yet. If you return the compliments, address to, Bakery Dept, Co-op Stores, Cramlington, from (Linesman) R. Turnbull.'

Mr Turnbull appears to have been an official at the local football matches and to have worked at Cramlington Co-op. The Cramlington Society had been in existence for over forty years when this card was sent. As well as a bakery, it boasted grocery, boot and shoe, butchery, hardware etc. The image is printed on light blue card and has no publisher's name.

This card was sent to Felling on Tyne in 1905. In pencil is written 'Cramlington Co-operative Society'. The number on the harness suggests a competition, which would be held on the village green adjacent to the Travellers Rest. This is Dudley Lane – the land behind the wall to the right is where the cinema has been built.

A nice card in the 'Alexandra Series' sent to Belford in 1908. The image shows the fashion at the time for glass domes enclosing floral tributes. The two small holly trees, on the left, are now splendidly mature.

The village in 1908 – The building in the centre of the photograph appears to have been built as two houses, one of which has been turned into a small shop. It was quite common for retail premises to begin in someone's front room.

This card was sent to Madame Richard in Paris in 1908. It is in the 'Alexandra Series' and the original has been nicely coloured. The view of the village must have been taken from the attic window of the Post Office.

CRAMLINGTON HALL

The view of the Old Hall is quite common but this card, sent to Miss M. Guillan, Pennsylvania, USA is particularly interesting. The card was written by Mr. J.H. Bodger, at that time the owner of the hall, who names himself and the other figures standing by the window between the two trees to the left of the image. I will quote the message (only a few words I cannot decipher) as it gives a little social insight into the times:

'Dear M. Aug. 4. 03. I received the paper giving account of great floods for which I thank you and in return send you a picture of the hall, Mr Jones, Mr Walton Postmaster and myself are standing beside sitting room window. Mrs B and children were away or would also have figured hereon. They are going to Alnwick this year. I have had a holiday in Warwickshire, my brother Dr Bodger's place … has been through the operation and is alright now. My brother Fred sailed to Canada last week for a month's holiday. Nancie is now being taught by Miss Cargey who comes from Benton every afternoon, she is now having her holidays and will be writing to you soon. Since writing this I see that it cannot be sent abroad so must enclose it in an envelope. I don't expect that you will ever return to the Old Country again, if you did you would not settle, as a rule people don't. That young man who has long been an … is still so. I think he would be worth coming back for he belongs to a very nice family, but you know best. Perhaps you have already met with someone that you think is better than the Grocer, be sure that he is and then make the best of it. With Kind Regards from Mrs. B and myself, wishing you every good wish and prosperity. Your Truly J.H. Bodger.'

The 'paper' sent from Pennsylvania may have been that which gave an account of the floods in Connellsville, Pennsylvania on 26th May 1902. The great storm passed over the area and torrential rain swelled the streams that fed the Breakneck Reservoir belonging to the Connellsville Water Company. The 'breast' of the reservoir was breached by the weight of water which swept down the valley destroying bridges, flooding farms, properties and damaging rail tracks. Apart from some farm animals no other casualties were reported.

'Miss Cargey' who travelled from Benton every afternoon to teach Nancie, probably came by train to Cramlington Station. Rail Services at that time were quite sophisticated as they were actually operated for the benefit of the public. The many branch lines served small communities like Cramlington giving regular and frequent services.

John Henry Bodger died at Cheltenham on 16th January 1949, aged 90 years, wife Ann, died on 26th August 1931, aged 70 years. Daughter Kathleen Elsie Allan died at Sheffield on 27th August 1978, aged 80 years and Nancie Bodger died 3rd April 1973, aged 79 years. All are buried in Cramlington churchyard within sight of their former home.

Post Office & Church, Cramlington.

This delightful view of Cramlington Village square was published by Robson Brothers, their premises are in the centre of the image, and posted in March 1912. The recipient was Sergt. John Crawford, Newburn Cottage, Newburn, Northumberland and reads:

'I thank you very much for your trouble in paying over my insurance SGNT, the receipt for same. Hope you are keeping well, glad to say we are. Wishing the strike was settled, we are very quiet, only a bit trouble with the boys riding the ponies. Will perhaps see you next Wed. I am all yours Russell.'

This card was written at the time of the 1912 National Coal Strike which appeared to be a direct result of a complicated wage situation. Miners were paid on a sliding scale which related wages directly to the selling price of coal. In the late 1890s this system was abandoned for wages calculated on the 'local price list'. Negotiated between the Miners' Federation and mine owners, payment was augmented by a percentage agreed by a Conciliation Board under an independent chairman. There were other considerations given to the miners such as working wet, variations in the seam of coal, occurrences of stone etc. These sums were usually fixed but the whole system made earning a fair and sustainable wage very difficult. In October 1911 the Miners' Federation resolved to secure an individual minimum wage to be negotiated for each district. Each was asked to prepare schedules of minimum rates for each grade of labour. A top rate of 8 shillings was asked by Yorkshire for hewers but the Federation settled on 7/6. The mine owners rejected all proposals and the national ballot that followed voted for a stoppage by over 50% of members.

By March 1912, it was clear through meetings that there was a strong feeling from the men for a return to work. The strike ended shortly before Easter with the passing of the Minimum Wage Act, to settle with the miners in their own districts – this essentially gave victory to the mine owners. In those days under strike conditions police and sometimes the Army were drafted into areas where trouble had occurred or was likely to happen. Cramlington had a bit of a reputation gained from the disturbances during the local miners' strike in 1865. Our card may have been sent by a police officer to his sergeant. The police presence would remain until the situation quieted down or a settlement of the strike was reached. The disturbances of 1865 were mainly sparked by the arrival of the 'Candy men' from Newcastle. These people were employed by the mine owners to evict miners and their families from the cottages they rented from the mine company. Further disturbances at this time happened with the arrival of Cornish miners and their families. They were recruited by the mine owners to work in place of the strikers. Cramlington then was probably looked upon as a risk to public order and a police presence was thought necessary. The writer of the card reports that all is quiet apart from boys riding the ponies. Presumably these were pit ponies (Pit Galawas) that had been taken out of the mines and put out to graze in the open air for the duration of the strike. An interesting card connected to a national event.

A view of Cramlington from the east published by Robson Brothers of Cramlington in 1913. It is unusual to note that all of the buildings shown here are still standing.

CRAMLINGTON. 1132.

Looking east from 'Doctor's Corner' towards High Pit, circa 1910. The Vicarage gates are seen on the right of the image.

Another splendid card, originally printed in colour, in the 'Alexandra Series' from 1907. Notice the height of the banking above the path on the right. This remained quite high until the re-development of the land lowered it to its present level. Some of the remaining stones in the bank side are still in place today.

Station Rd. & Post Office, Cramlington.

A postcard by R. Johnston of Gateshead looking towards the station, showing the original Railway Tavern on the far left. All of the buildings in the view have been demolished. The card was sent to Workington in Cumberland in 1915.

Another card in the 'Monarch Series' by R. Johnston & Sons. The card was sent unaddressed so, could have been in an envelope or parcel.

The card reads: 'Do let me know about Tom if all well, by letter. We have to go to the morning parade now but I am still in the ... Also top coats and all need to be packed in our bags and one blanket and waterproof sheet, all ready to go in the trenches in case of an air raid. I will write again Thursday. Love to all, we are copping it now, real hot hell. Best Love George x.'

George sent the view of Blagdon Terrace to 'Dearest Aenid' sometime after 1915 and he was probably a soldier in the Northumberland Fusiliers. Air raids by Zeppelins became more frequent in the North after the first raid on the coast in April 1915. The fact that his kit had to be kept ready to move at a moment's notice demonstrates that the Zeppelins' threat was considered serious and imminent. The issue of the top coat, one blanket and a waterproof sheet seems pitifully inadequate given, our knowledge of the horror George was to face in France.

The sender of this card gives information regarding the arrival of the Duke of Cornwall's Light Infantry at Cramlington. It was posted on 19th November 1914, to Mrs H.H. Jenkin, Churchtown, St Stephen, Cornwall and reads:

The Church, Cramlington.

'Dear Bean, we are at Cramlington now. We marched from Newcastle here this morning, about 10 miles, it is in the county of Northumberland. I don't know how long we shall be here. I can't give you any address as I don't know myself. I will try to write to you a letter sometime of the day if I have got time. I am alright; don't worry, with best love H.H.J.'

Marching 10 miles with full packs must have been quite an ordeal for 'H.H.' and his comrades but a real treat for the locals as the regiment passed through their village.

Cramlington, Winter.

The inscription on the reverse of this card gives the date 'Christmas 1915' and identifies the soldiers as those belonging to the Duke of Cornwall's Light Infantry. The man on the extreme right is identified as Bob Oliver, a local man who was known by my father. The regiment was billeted in Cramlington School. This card has not been postally used, is a little creased here and there but bears a well composed image of soldiers who may have spent their next Christmas in the trenches.

**Thinking
of you
at
Cramlington.**

I think of you by night,
I think of you by day,
In fact my head is full of thinks,
When you are far away.

I find this card intriguing as it gives rise to conjecture of the romantic kind. In the 'Regent Series' and printed in England by Regent Publishing, London, the publishers state in bold capital letters that the card is 'All British'.

The card was sent to 'Corporal Dowrick, 6 Henry Street, Bodmin, Cornwall'. The date given is '29th 1915' (no month) and reads: 'Dear Corporal I thank you for the nice cards you sent me. When are you coming back, Miriam.'

Thirteen kisses tell of Miriam's affection for the good Corporal who would have been a soldier in the Duke of Cornwall's Light Infantry, billeted in Cramlington School at the time. Was Miriam an amour of Corporal Dowrick – a local lass who fell for a soldier? Or, as the writing suggests, was she a school girl with a crush on the gallant defender of the realm. Miriam's message is respectful and direct but without the familiarity of a lover. The thirteen kisses however, betray great affection. The final mystery is whether the corporal ever received the card as the green half penny stamp is not cancelled.

The village green does look a bit muddy in this view of 1912. West Farm buildings are at the right with the conical roof of the gin gan clearly visible. The roof windows of the post office were used to take photographs of the village. The shop and terrace on the left were owned by Cramlington Co-op society.

An interior view of the Primitive Methodist Church looking like the harvest festival celebration. My father always had fond memories of the 'Welcome' and I was christened here in 1951.

P. M. Church, Station Terrace Cramlington. 1910

CRAMLINGTON VICARAGE. 1135.

A rare image of Cramlington Church Vicarage. The Vicarage garden contained apple, plum and pear trees which every autumn became a target for local ruffians like me. My cousin, Michael Parker and I were 'hired' by the vicar's son one year to protect the trees from thieves. The gentle soul of course, had not the slightest inking that he was allowing the wolves to look after the sheep.

This card by Johnston was sent from 57 Station Road in 1915 to Ryton. The image shows a gathering of soldiers, a splendid old car and a few locals looking on. The houses have changed little over the years. Johnston often placed his car in clear view while taking his photographs – is that his vehicle featured here?

Station Road, Cramlington 2579.

West View, Cramlington

Above: A card in the 'Alexandra Series' looking towards 'Doctor's Corner' and the Vicarage along Blagdon Terrace in 1914. The building at the left is the Mechanics' Institute and the original form of the church yard wall can clearly be seen.

Left: A closer view of the Mechanics' Institute, opened by Lady Ridley in December 1894. Since then it has been used for various purposes, including a branch of a bank. Currently, the building is being converted into living accommodation.

This view has changed little except for the Post Office building in centre distance. An unsent card by Robson Brothers, circa 1915.

Blagdon Hotel, Cramlington.

Station Road, Cramlington.

Station Road – The building with the tall chimney on the right of the image is a part of the Cramlington Co-operative Society Central Buildings. An unsent card by Robson Brothers, circa 1915.

An unusual view of Cramlington in the Auty Series, circa 1910. The large house on the right was built in 1905. Cramlington Hall can be seen through the trees on the extreme left and the Vicarage garden sports a white painted dovecot mounted on a pole. The grass in the foreground is now covered by the Allensgreen Estate.

Cramlington Church and Vicarage

2276

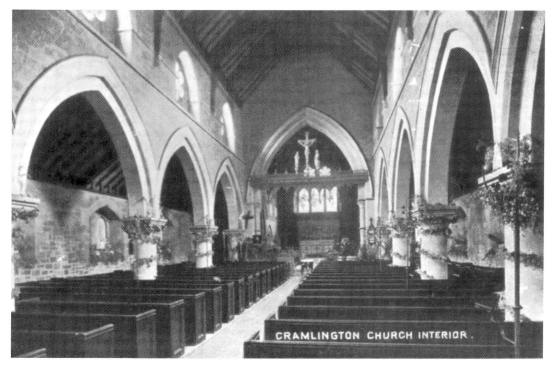

CRAMLINGTON CHURCH INTERIOR.

Cramlington Church interior – the sender of this card in 1908, tells Mrs Gardiner in Newcastle that he 'had a four mile walk before breakfast this morning'. A nice interior view of the church by an unknown publisher.

15

Cramlington At War

This card was received by Miss A. Davison, from an expectant Drummer E. Firth, 16th Service Battalion, Northumberland Fusiliers. The card was published by Solomon Brothers and is No 213 in their series. There is no address for Miss Davison, it may have been sent by envelope or regimental post.

The Drummer writes: 'Dear Annie, you're welcome letter to hand, I am to understand that there is no weekend leave this week, so if convenient would like to see you on Sunday, with love to all, Ernest Firth.'

The Battalion was officially recognised by the War Office on 8th September 1914 but was in existence before this date. Early in 1915 the '16th' was rushed to Cramlington by special train from Alnwick. A German landing on the North East coast was feared and this was confirmed in the minds of the men by the issue of live ammunition. On arrival at Cramlington the battalion was forced to spend the night in the open until tents could be pitched and a proper camp set up, next day – and of course it rained all night! Nothing changes.

The reason for the sudden deployment was not imminent invasion by 'Fritzy' – it was that he could if he so wished. Coastal defences at this time were manned by the territorials but they had gone overseas leaving the coast wide open to any unwelcome visitors. Someone, somewhere suddenly realised that the coast has been left open and panic ensued, only you cannot associate panic with the British Army. The transfer was done with flags flying, bands playing and the military precision and organisation in which the Army has always excelled. No doubt, however, someone, somewhere, was greatly relieved when the '16th' marched into Cramlington. The trenches and defences (which had been prepared earlier by the 1st Tyneside Pioneers) were said to be rudimentary. The art of trench digging and bunker building, perfected by the German Army, was in its infancy and these trenches could only be manned in 'shifts' with soldiers returning to camp or to billets. The value of the whole North East Coast Defence system is still a matter of controversy. On 23rd June 1915, the battalion left Cramlington for Catterick Bridge and arrived at Boulogne on 22nd November.

R. Johnston produced this image of Cramlington Council Schools sometime in 1915. The same building housed a junior school downstairs and senior upstairs and this was still so when I started there in 1956. A small boy looks through the railings at the soldiers mustering in the school yard. By this time uniformed, full equipped and armed soldiers would have been a common sight in Cramlington. These soldiers belong to the Duke of Cornwall Light

Infantry who were billeted here in 1915. Sent to Miss May Fairlamb, Witton Gilbert, Durham. The card reads: 'Dear May Annie will send you a PC tomorrow. Did your uncle get down to help you this morning? Hope it keeps fine for you. Love from Aunt Annie.'

Top right: A composition card by R. Johnston posted in 1915, shortly after a Zeppelin raid on Cramlington. Each of the photographs on the cards were postcards in their own right.

Bottom right: 'Somewhere' was probably the Camp at Plessey Bridge; the area now occupied by the travellers' caravan park.

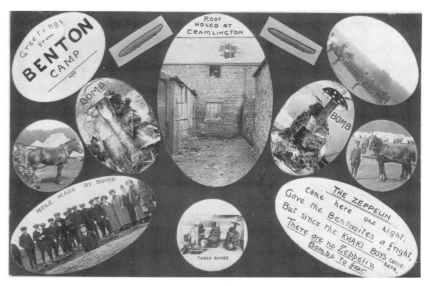

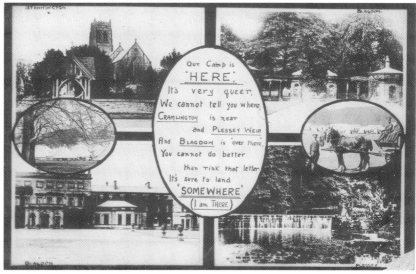

The 18th Service Battalion Northumberland Fusiliers was created in February of 1915. In April of that year they left Rothbury for Cramlington by special train and on arrival camped overnight in a field close to the station. Initially the Battalion, also known as the 1st Tyneside Pioneers, were engaged in constructing a line of defences between Cramlington and the coast. The Battalion became part of the North Eastern Coast Defence Force and these defences eventually linked with those dug nearer the coast to become known as 'Fitton's Line'. Major General Fitton, whom the defences were named after, was killed in France in 1916. It was felt that any German force landed with the intention of threatening Newcastle industries, would be held by 'Fitton's Line' of defences. To complete its work the Battalion was forced to approach local collieries for the loan of picks and shovels to augment its inadequate supply. It is reported that the collieries responded favourably but expected the return of their tools – the Battalion fulfilled this expectation. Shortly before the arrival of the 18th, a German Zeppelin had crossed the coast causing a bit of a stir. The Zeppelin raid on Cramlington and surrounding areas on 14th April 1915 is recorded as being only the second ever air raid on Britain. The first was on the night of 19th/20th January 1915 over Norfolk when Kapitan Hans Fritz bombed Yarmouth.

At 7 pm on 14th April the Zeppelin airship L9, commanded by Kapitan-Leutnant Mathy appeared off the mouth of the Tyne. The L9 had been keeping an eye on British shipping in the North Sea and Mathy had gained permission to unload his bombs on the Tyne industries. Travelling north to Blyth he then turned inland with the intention of attacking the industrial areas of Tyneside. The 1st Battalion Northern Cyclists were stationed at Cambois and the L9 was met by their ineffective rifle fire. The first bomb was dropped on a field at West Sleekburn. Further bombs were dropped at Bedlington and Cramlington and two casualties were caused by bombs at Wallsend. A women and child were slightly injured, little damage was caused.

Left: Northern Cyclist Battalion (E Company) at Drill.

The gathering of locals in Choppington High Street seen to be dividing their attention between the photographer and the cardboard Zeppelin drifting overhead. The image has obviously been faked – shame on you Robert Johnston of Gateshead. The voice of the photographer can almost be heard telling the crowd to 'look up and point', just before the shutter clicked. This card is postally unused, is in quite poor condition but remains a scarce 'record' of the event.

Zeppelin Visit to Choppington, 14th. April, 1915.

Zeppelin Visit to Blyth, 14th April 1915

A view of the market place, Bridge Street in Blyth. The Zeppelin is a little more convincing than the Choppington effort but no one is looking skywards. This card was sent to a Miss M. Little of Havant, Hampshire and reads: 'Dear Mabs, thanks for the letter this evening. I am rather busy and not much time to write but hope to have a bit more time tomorrow. I finished the mat tonight and I am sending five along tomorrow. This is a P.C of the Zep raid over this part of the globe; this is the one that came over the camp. They have been paying short visits to places close to here. But not happened to come here. I will be sure and send the mats on tomorrow for certain. I must knock of now as I have got to clean up for the guard tomorrow. So long, from Biff.'

Biff gives himself away as being a soldier, probably in the Hampshire Regiment and stationed in one of the camps in the Blyth/Cramlington area. He mentions guard duty and also, interesting, mats. I think we can presume that Biff was a proponent of the ancient art of 'clippy' or 'proggy' mat making. A backing material with an open weave would be stretched on a frame being whatever size you wanted the mat to be. Coloured material was cut into strips and woven into the backing material creating colourful patterns and a hard wearing tread mat. This traditional craft was still current during the 1950s and I remember my grandmother patiently producing wonderfully coloured mats that lasted for years. Biff obviously kept himself busy in camp between duties by working on his mats, taking a great deal of care and pride in their production.

It can only be imagined what consternation and curiosity this huge cigar shaped monster created as it crossed the skies of the North East. The images of the Blyth, Choppington and Bedlington cards have obviously been contrived. No doubt many of these cards were sold as a record of the event, even if they were fakes! By contrast today there would be thousands of images, courtesy of everyone's mobile phones! Alongside these mock up cards are those which show bomb damage, craters, buildings etc. The best of these, quite scarce images were produced by yes you guessed it R. Johnston, who issued well studied sharp images in real photography form.

It looks like half the population of Bedlington have taken the opportunity to have their photograph taken for free. It is interesting to note that the young lads seated around the rim of the crater are dressed in the same manner as their elders who are standing. At this time childhood did not last that long and the entry into the adult world of work came much earlier than today.

Another fake Zeppelin postcard – this time at Bedlington.

This card depicts what looks to be a farm building in Bell's Yard, Cramlington. This was situated directly opposite the Golden Dragon and adjacent to the Lal Qila. An incendiary bomb has pierced the roof and caused quite a bit of damage with the resulting fire. Another superb image by Johnston which was sent to Mrs Stirk, Agill Cottage, Heselton, Bedale and reads: 'Dear Mrs Stirk, just a PC to let you know I arrived safe. I got home at 15 to 8. This is the Zeppelin raid that was here. From your friend Ellen.'

The chap on the right is equipped to fill in the hole left by the dastardly 'Hun' in farmer Turnbull's field. Robert Johnston, the photographer, has not attracted much of a crowd in this scene. Without the information on the card it could be thought that this chap is proudly displaying a hole he has just dug.

When I was a young chap this type of dress was still current with the older men of the village – suits with waistcoats,

collarless shirts, watch chains and flat caps – this photograph could have been taken in the 1950s.

Robert Johnston was again on hand to record the remains of the incendiary devices dropped by the L9. They are quite crude but nonetheless effective in causing curiosity which quickly turned to dread as the number of raids increased and casualties mounted. The bombs presumably detonated on impact and were primed before being dropped. The remains of what appears to be rope are wound

ZEPPELIN RAID. APRIL 14th, 1915.
Explosive bombs dropped. (Z2)

around the central core, incendiary material on top of this and the whole encased in metal. What is absolutely clear is that these bombs were dropped by hand from the Gondola of the L9 as carrying handles can be clearly seen in the image.

The Zeppelin L9 Specifications were:

Length:	529 ft 4ins	Diameter Maximum:	52 ft 5 ins
Gas Volume:	879,500 square ft	Number of gas cells:	15
Gondolas:	2	Propellers:	3 Lorenzen
Maximum speed:	53 mph	Range:	1,750 miles
Ceiling:	9,000 ft	Payload:	24,450 lbs
Empty weight:	39,200 lbs	Engines:	3 x Maybach CX (210 hp each, 630 hp total
Factory No:	LZ 36	Yard:	Friedrichshafenl
Maiden Flight:	8th March 1915 – 74 scouting missions, 4 raids		
Burned:	16th September 1916		

An object which is 529 feet long is difficult to imagine. However, if the L9 were stood on end next to Cramlington Church Tower it would be more than seven times its height. How the 1st Cyclists at Cambois managed to miss the damned thing is a mystery. Perhaps they were riding their bikes at the time.

In der Zeppelin-Gondel

This German 'Feldpost' card was sent to Strasbourg on 28th January 1915 by a German airman. It depicts the gondola of a Zeppelin and looks to be about 30ft long and 8ft to 10ft wide. There is a glazed canopy forward and searchlights are fitted to help detect ground targets. Bombs would be dropped by hand so the whole process was a little hit and miss. A lot of raids were carried out at night and unless the craft was stationery over its target, the 'barn door' was as safe as houses. The Zeppelins effectiveness as a weapon of war was negligible but the psychological impact upon the civilian population must have been great.

This card by Smith of Hull is black edged for mourning and depicts an artist's impression of a raid on 15th June 1915, in which 16 were killed and 40 injured. This card is postally unused and the title 'The Midnight Assassin' suggests the dastardly 'Hun' at his fiendish worst. Killing innocent civilians in their own beds was not the British way of making war. The German air force had created a new way of warfare in which those on the ground could not protect themselves.

This card, published by Albert Ebner, Munich and posted in Stuttgart on 16th September 1914, is in stark contrast to the Midnight Assassin card. The Zeppelin and its crew are depicted as heroes and are cheered by the German people. This artist's impression shows a Zeppelin craft bombing Liittich (Liege, Belgium) during the siege of that city in August 1914.

A little over a year since the first Zeppelin raids on the North East coastal towns, the Stonefield Series of West Hartlepool published this card with the title 'Strafed'. Defences had significantly improved and the great airships were vulnerable to ground anti-aircraft fire and particularly so against the nimble flying machines of the Royal Flying Corps. The card is postally unused and depicts a Zeppelin caught in searchlights, plunging to fiery destruction in the North Sea having been strafed by concentrated ground fire on 27th November 1916.

Flying At Cramlington

This 'two view' card of Cramlington was sent to Kirkaldy in Fife, Scotland on 29th April 1917. It reads: 'Dear Sarah, Wednesday night very busy working last night and tonight. Flying tomorrow night, this will do you until I get time to give you letter. I got your letter yesterday, scones etc. and today your PC. Don't be angry, keep smiling every circus has a clown you know, as has A.J. more than one sometimes. I hope R – will have a good holiday and glad to hear John is O.K. Had a letter today from Cunningham, he is not going to Egypt now. Had a wee bit flee on Saturday afternoon. Will give you letter as soon as possible very well. Hope you are all in the pink. Lots of love, yours aye Bob.'

There are a few clues in the message that may reveal the true nature of 'aye Bob'. Firstly he was a Scot who had a 'wee bit flee' (a short flight to you and me). Secondly, he liked scones and thirdly, he may have been a pilot at the RFC station at Cramlington.

Cramlington Royal Flying Corps station was built in 1915 as a direct response to earlier Zeppelin raids on the North East coast. The station was built to the west of the village by what older residents of Cramlington still know as the 'aerodrome road'. This is the road that runs from Shaw's Garden Centre to Plessey Checks. A flight of two BE2cs was formed on 1st December 1915, with another added shortly after. This became known as the Tyneside Home Defence Flight, which was absorbed into 36 Squadron 8th Wing, VI Training Brigade on 1st February 1916. The Cramlington unit was re-designated 36 (Home Defence) Squadron in November/December 1917. On 1st January 1918, Cramlington became a training airfield and from 1st April 1918, under the newly formed RAF, an operational training airfield.

Aye Bob's card is dated April 1917 which would make him a trainee pilot in the 36 (Home Defence) Squadron.

Left: This is a photograph of an Armstrong Whitworth FK8 A2723 taken inside its hangar at Cramlington, circa 1918.

Left: Three Hawker Horsley Aircraft of the 36 (Home Defence) Squadron at Cramlington. The eagle gripping a torpedo in its talons on the tail of the aircraft is the Squadron insignia and the motto is: 'Ralawi Raja Langit' which means 'Eagle King of the Sky'.

In October 1919, service flying came to an end at Cramlington with the disbanding of 52 Training Squadron. The station was used for storage until final closure in January 1920. The Cramlington Aircraft Company established itself at the airfield in 1921/22, operating aircraft like the Gypsy and Simmonds Spartan. After the demise of the company the airfield fell into disrepair. In 1925 the Newcastle Aeroclub took over the site and its first task was to build a new hangar. The club stayed at Cramlington for 10 years until the site was officially closed.

Once again Robert Johnston of Gateshead visited Cramlington in the 1920s. On this particular day he took these two wonderful photographs right of planes flying at the Aerodrome.

Right: A Johnston postcard titled 'Flying at Cramlington'. Is that the photographer's car appearing in the picture again?

In the 1930s, during the time of Newcastle Aeroclub, my grandparents lived in the clubhouse on the field. My father always spoke fondly of his time at the 'Aerodrome' as it was known to the locals. Being a 'young lad' it was his task to look after the goats, geese and chickens. Obviously quite a chore. To make up, however, he got to drive the 'Chassis'. This was an old car that had been stripped down to nothing but wheels, chassis, engine and seat. It was used to tow the gliders down the grass runway to get them airborne.

After the field closed in 1935 the facility was still in use. My father says that during the early years of the Second World War, naval ordinance was stored in the abandoned hangars. He would tell the story of the night a jittery army sentry who fired his 303 at a cyclist who did not respond to his challenge. Whether they were armed or warning shots my father did not say, only that the cyclist shot off as though motorized.

My aunt Olive Parker (née Godfrey) with Rex and the fearsome 'Nanny' the 'watch goat' in front of Cramlington Aerodrome clubhouse in the late 1930s.

This envelope sent to Cramlington Aerodrome on 11th December 1939, contained details of the re scheduling / cancellation of flights and also the same information on the railways in Holland. The situation in Europe at this time was uncertain to say the least but contacts were maintained as long as possible.

My Norwegian grandmother outside Cramlington Gliding clubhouse in the late 1930s.

Cramlington Aerodrome had a distinguished visitor with the arrival of Sir Alan Cobham's Flying Circus in the mid 1930s (show above). Cobham's National Aviation Day displays began in 1932 and he and his pilots and planes, usually a dozen or more various types of aircraft, would tour the country. Flights were offered to the public in a bi-plane for six shillings – about a week's wage in those days. Displays were put on at hundreds of locations throughout the year. Any location from established airfields to a decent stretch of flat grass was used and the crowds flocked to see the show. Aerial acrobatics, wing walkers, low flying, and all the elements of traditional 'barnstorming' excitement no doubt made for a memorable day. Cobham of course was just the chap for this sort of flying. An RFC pilot during the war, a pioneer of long distance flying and a test pilot for de Havilland was quite a pedigree.

Of course, the most famous and celebrated flyer of the time and probably in the whole history of flight, also visited the aerodrome. Major Bigglesworth late of the Royal Flying Corps was the sort of chap you would be glad to have on your side in a tight corner. It was at Cramlington Aerodrome that the major and Algy and Ginger found themselves after escaping from a gang of Russians who were up to no good. Needless to say the Russians, who were thoroughly bad eggs by the way, were thwarted in their design by the good Major and his companions. They stayed at Cramlington for only a few days planning how to defeat the Black Peril. Strange, my father did not mention he knew 'Biggles'.

Right: The front cover of 'Biggles and the Black Peril' by Capt W.E. Johns. The Biggles books were very popular between the two world wars and in this book the famous pilot visits Cramlington Aerodrome.

Another response to the threat of coastal attack was the construction of an airship hanger at Nelson Village. It is seen in these three photographs in a state of demolition in 1968. Originally intended to house four small airships which would augment the Home Defence Squadron, the 'shed', as it was known locally, was never used for this purpose. Ammunition boxes were made here during the remainder of the First World War and it was not until 1929 that the Airship Development Company used the shed's cavernous interior for its original purpose. They built a small airship that was used to advertise Walter Willson's Stores. This was at the time when the airship was very much in the public eye. The German Graf Zeppelin was regularly crossing the Atlantic to South America, carrying passengers. The R100 and R101 were being built in this country and Italy, Norway and America, among others, were also making pioneering efforts.

During the Second World War, lorries were built here from parts brought in from the USA. After the war a coach building firm used the shed until its final occupier was a firm making concrete lamp posts. The size of the place can be gauged by noting the dimensions of the great hanger doors, measuring 120 feet by 80 feet and each weighing more than 30 tons. This huge landmark, which overshadowed Nelson Village and regularly disrupted its electricity supply, was dismantled in 1968. The great doors, considered to be the largest mechanically operated hanger doors in the country, were removed first. The shell was 'sliced', almost like a loaf of bread, with cutting torches and pulled down a slice at a time. A cable was attached to a girder and to a bulldozer and tons of rusting, twisted metal were ready to cart off for scrap. The fall of each section produced a brown rust cloud at ground level and a black cloud of bats as their roost was destroyed. The sad demise of a wonderful but dangerous playground for us kids!

The Flying Scotsman

Probably the most well known image of the 1926 Flying Scotsman derailment although it is technically a 'card from Cramlington' it is not an original image, being a modern reprint.

In May 1926 with the General Strike in full swing, some Cramlington miners removed a rail from the up line Berwick to Newcastle. Their intention was to stop trains pulling coal which they considered 'blackleg'. This term is essentially mining in origin. As miners usually wore 'hoggers' or shorts while working underground, legs would naturally get dirty. Striking miners would presumably have clean legs so any that showed dust would be 'black legs' or strike breakers. The story of the derailment is too well known to go into detail, suffices to say that the coal train did not arrive but the Scotsman did, and pulled by the engine 'Merry Hampton'.

The following is a transcript of the original three page report on the incident written by Joseph Henry Mcilvenna. The original documents are type written and faded on the paper which is fragile and tissue like. A small hand drawn map of the area plotting Mr Mcilvenna's findings was once attached but now unfortunately lost.

Joseph Henry Mcilvenna states:

'I reside at No 6 Elysium Lane, Bensham, Gateshead. I am a Chartered Civil Engineer and I am Assistant District Engineer for the Northumberland District in the employment of the London North Eastern Railway Company. The main line of the London and North Eastern Railway Company between Newcastle and Berwick is included in my district.

'I hand in a plan drawn to scale of 1/2500 ordnance showing the main line and what adjoins it at the east side in the neighbourhood of West Cramlington. It is a double line protected from the adjoining fields by post and rail fences. The metals, which are of the 95 lb weight to the yard type, are each 45 feet in length, are fixed into iron chairs with Oak wood keys, and secured to the preceding and succeeding rails by pairs of steel fish plates, eighteen inches long, through which and the rails are fish bolts which are secured by fish bolt nuts. The chairs are each approximately 49 lb in weight, are fixed by two six inch steel spikes and two six-and-a-half inch trenails to wood sleepers each nine feet by ten inches by five inches, and of which there are seventeen to the 45 feet length. The sleepers are laid on stone ballast which is of a general depth of six inches.'

'On Monday, 10th May 1926, I received a report and went to what is locally known as West Cramlington Junction on the main North line and arrived there about 3 pm. I there saw an engine and five passenger coaches derailed from the 'up' line. The point of derailment is: 1,016 yards north of Dam Dykes signal cabin and 1,148 yards south of Cramlington signal cabin, and 275 yards south of no 57 bridge – all as shown on the plan which I have handed in. I at once examined the 'up' line at the point of derailment and found that one length of rail – the outside rail – was completely out of position, but held tightly by ballast and pressure from the frame or bogie of derailed restaurant car no 64435. Later I had this rail cleared and with Permanent Way Inspector Penberthy, examined it was clean, straight and undamaged. All the other outside rails of the 'up' line over the area of derailment were in a twisted condition and there were several breaks. The inner corresponding rail with the loose straight rail was within the jaws of its chairs, but all the wood keys were missing. The fish plates and fish bolts and nuts, with the exception of one broken fish bolt produced, which was lying in the four foot way were missing. The remaining part of this bolt, with nut screwed on, was picked up later. The nut produced shows the indentations of heavy, presumably, hammer blows. The fish plate produced was lying near. The rail end which terminated the sound track at the point of derailment showed on the outside face of the top flange new bright indentations apparently from heavy hammer blows aimed at the nut of the fish bolt. The fish bolt and nut produced with the nut partially threaded on, I saw picked up from the grass immediately opposite the joint and it was handed to me. The other fish bolt produced, I saw similarly picked up and it was handed to me.

'I saw wood keys floating on the surface of a marshy pond 20 feet outside the boundary fence and I sent a man to gather them. I saw him do that and he brought twenty seven keys and the fish bolt nut produced. On my instruction a search was made in some bushes just outside the boundary fence and I saw Permanent Way Inspector Penberthy take from underneath a bush: one fish plate showing hammer marks, one sledge hammer marked 'OLD' on one side and 'N.E.R' on the other, one platelayer's pinch bar, one screw key which fits the fish bolt nuts. I took possession of the tools which are similar to those used by our platelayers and produce them. In my opinion the derailment was caused by the removal of fish plates and keys, and as the particular rail which I have referred to as having been found out of position, was in no way damaged I conclude that it had been toppled out of the chairs.'

Right: The locomotive 'Merry Hampton' that was derailed at Cramlington in 1926. It is seen here a year later at Inveresk on its way to Newcastle. Rebuilt in 1945, the 'Merry Hampton' was in service until 1963.

I think we would agree that Mr Mcilvenna was very thorough in his investigation of the site. Even to the untrained eye, the evidence would suggest a deliberate act of derailment and therefore a criminal and potentially murderous act. In the event, injuries to passengers were only cuts, bruises and shock. In his wonderful little book of memories from the time Billy Muckle, who was directly involved in the derailment, is naturally scathing of the treatment received by the miners but had no regrets for his actions. As a young man, I knew Billy Muckle and Tommy Roberts, who both lived in Nelson Village and were both nice men who had done desperate deeds in desperate times.

Pigeons and Pigeon Men

This card was actually sent from Carlisle on 1st September 1919. It was sent to W.H Endean of Laurel Cottages, Cramlington. The photograph shows a 'fancier' standing proudly beside his magnificent pigeon lofts presumably in Carlisle. The card reads:

'Dear Sir, I received the hen safely on Saturday afternoon, thanks for trouble. I will let her out tomorrow Tuesday. If she arrives again please keep her and advise me. Will write you later. Yours Truly.'

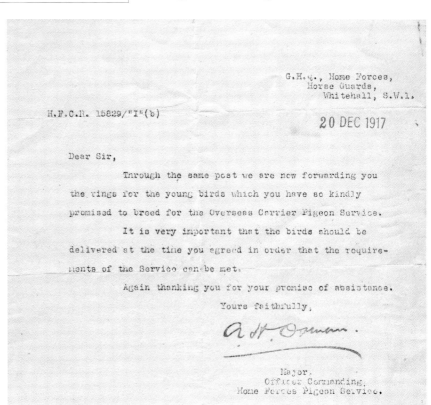

LAUREL LOFTS.

PURE BARKERS!
PURE BARKERS!!
PURE BARKERS!!!

Owing to the restrictions on Racing in this district, we are open to book SQUEAKERS for 1917. Our Stock Birds have flown successfully **Troyes, Arlon** (600 miles), **Chimay, Mons** (400 and 500 miles). This loft is noted for the famous **Barkers**, also Nisbets (Galston). Our Racers are the Show Birds—our Show Birds are the Racers. No separate lofts.

Price 10/- each.

Money returned in full if not satisfied. **2/6** deposit when booking.

APPLY **ENDEAN & RINGWOOD,**
Laurel Cottages, Cramlington, *via* Newcastle-on-Tyne, Northumberland.

Our man from Carlisle had bought the hen pigeon from Endean and Ringwood, Laurel Lofts, Laurel Cottages. Laurel Lofts according to their advertisement was noted for its 'Barkers' and also 'Nisbets' – 'Stock birds have flown successfully to Troyes Arlon (600 miles), Chimay, Mons (400 & 500 miles)'.

The price for these little beauties in 1917 was ten shillings each with a half crown deposit on booking.

Left: An advert for Laurel Lofts, Laurel Cottages, Cramlington.

Right: A letter from GHQ Home Forces, sent to Laurel Cottages.

GHQ Home Forces published a list of the birds that accompanied the British Expeditionary Force into Belgium and France in 1914/15. The birds are not given names (although their handlers probably did give them names) but are recognised by the letters and numbers on their leg rings. The list simply gives the number, colour and sex of the bird and records in excess of 500 pigeons.

No. 1241 GHQ 1916 – Blue Cock – was bred by Endean and Ringwood at the Laurel Lofts, Cramlington.

G.H.Q., Home Forces,
Horse Guards,
Whitehall, S.W.1.

H.F.C.R. 15829/"I"(b)

20 DEC 1917

Dear Sir,

Through the same post we are now forwarding you the rings for the young birds which you have so kindly promised to breed for the Overseas Carrier Pigeon Service.

It is very important that the birds should be delivered at the time you agreed in order that the requirements of the Service can be met.

Again thanking you for your promise of assistance.

Yours faithfully,

Major,
Officer Commanding,
Home Forces Pigeon Service.

The North of England has been the virtual homeland of pigeon fancying for many years so it was inevitable that the military would call upon breeders to provide birds, for what was then, a vital means of communication. This is confirmed by the Air Ministry in 1919 by the publication of a booklet entitled, 'Homing Pigeons – Meritorious service in the Royal Air Force'. In its introduction the booklet states that the 'list' only includes birds which have performed conspicuously good service, but many other pigeons have also done consistently good work. Here are some examples of incidents in which pigeons played crucial roles in carrying messages:

60 NU 17 GPS	Cock	Seaplane down on water with engine trouble. First news came from pigeon message, and assistance was sent.
104 NU 17 GPS	Cock	Liberated from seaplane in difficulties, the message carried means of the saving of lives of the pilot and observer.
186 NU 17 GPS	Hen	Brought message that machine was forced to land, had crash and was sinking.
296 NU HP 16 SFC	Cock	Brought message saying machine on water, sinking when found, crew had been in water for over two hours sitting on the upturned floats.
485 NURP 17.F	Cock	The last bird to be liberated from a total wreck in 190 miles at sea on a dark stormy December night, with a 30-knot wind dead against him. He arrived at the loft with message early next morning.
1176 NU 18 GPS		Returned with message from airship, arriving at loft badly wounded in back.
2278 RP 17 EJ	Hen	Liberated from Short Seaplane with message 'landed owing to engine trouble returned with crop cut open.'
17291 NURP 17 F 17293 NURP 17F	Cock Cock	Helpless on the water the pilot and observer sent these pigeons with the following message: 'We can hear firing, but, cannot sea land or ships. Can you send round coast about 21 miles or so out. We really have no knowledge of our position at all. Very urgent both feeling very faint. Perhaps we are off the Southern Coast, Compass no use.'

These are only a very few incidents in which the natural instincts of these birds were relied upon and realised in the saving of lives. 'Pigeon Men' almost dedicated their lives to their birds, which are lovingly tended, proudly flown and deeply mourned. A way of life that has steadily declined over the years to were, it is uncommon to see a circling flight of a pigeon over allotment gardens.

The loft of Bob Hall of Blagdon.

The loft of Robert and Dick Fryer of Cramlington at the time of the First World War. Robert stands stiffly to attention while Dick strikes a typically heroic pose. Both hold prized birds instead of the splendid cup standing on the baskets.

This loft is proudly displayed, presumably by its owner and members of his family, circa 1918.

Cramlington Co-operative Society

It is not the intention here to recount the early history of the Society. The deeds of the founding members have been well documented on the Jubilee Souvenir History of Cramlington Co-operative Society published in 1912. The 'Store' employed hundreds of people in the Cramlington area. Eventually, branches were opened in Annitsford, West Moor, Seaton Burn, Dudley, Burradon, Dinnington and Wideopen, also Shank House, East Cramlington, High Pit and Nelson Village. In the days when it was not uncommon for a young chap to leave school on a Friday and begin working life on the Monday following I began my working life at the Annitsford branch of the Society. What is evident to me now is that common practises within the retail grocery trade of forty-five years age are in stark contrast of those today.

The Annitsford branch was a small, flat roofed, single storey building and had a drapery department next door, I do not remember too much about my short time here. The staff group was quite small, a couple of married ladies and a travelling shop driver. The branch had a long wooden counter fitted along three sides with the goods stacked on shelves around the walls, three cash drawers no tills. This kind of traditional set up provided the ultimate in personal service. Very often I have seen the shop full and spilling out onto the street with people waiting to be served. This would usually be on a Friday when the good ladies of Annitsford would do their traditional weekend shop – 'getting the groceries in' for the week ahead was an essential activity. Today shopping appears to be about a hobby for some who are happy to visit the 'Malls' daily. A shopper would arrive with a list of items if the list were written then the process would not take too long. Simply read from the list,

Seaton Burn Branch showing typical grocery, drapery and butchery shops – the following three photographs are other Cramlington Co-op branches.

Cramlington Co-op, High Pit Branch in the 1970s.

take the items from the shelves add up the prices take payment and issue a small receipt with the member's 'cheque number'. Each member had a number – my mother's was 767 – and a 'cheque' was issued with the amount after each purchase. This was duplicated by carbon paper and every three months the members dividends were calculated from the amount spent. Many thrifty housewives would simply allow their dividend to accumulate over the year. The money would then be put to good use at Christmas time or for new clothes at Easter. This was still the time when Easter was celebrated not only with chocolate eggs and bunnies but with new summer clothes – shirts and sandals for the boys and pretty dresses for the girls – the weather seemed so much better then though!

A visit to their local branch was a special occasion as well as a necessity for many. Very often chairs were provided for elderly customers and local news and gossip was rife. The relationship between server and customer was important. A lot of the older customers had favourite counter assistants for one reason or another. Some would be noted for giving 'good weight', others for being the source of all knowledge in village affairs and others simply because they were patient and pleasant. These criteria would apply to all branches.

Cramlington Colliery Branch of the Co-op with, to the right, the Primitive Methodist Church.

All branches had a 'laddie' – this was my position at Annitsford. One of my duties was to deliver grocery orders to the old folk living in the aged miners' cottages. There is something quite humbling in being in the company of old people. Most appreciated the company and looked forward to my regular visits. The stories they could tell – one old gentleman was with Allenby in Palestine and entered triumphant into Jerusalem in 1917 – amazing! Anyway a 'laddie' was required at the Dudley Branch and it was there that I directed my tread. The Dudley branch was a far bigger old imposing building. Built in two stories, retail areas at ground level with the traditional hall above. The building had suffered a fire that had destroyed the upper floor which was removed leaving only the shops below. Butchers, drapery and grocery became the combination in the larger branches and Dudley offered the shopper self-service and an electric till. At the rear were former stables that now housed the

Cramlington Co-op, Dudley Branch.

Smiths Electric mobile shops or 'vans' as we termed them, warehousing for fruit and vegetables, other small disused building and on incinerator – burning rubbish on a winters day was a fine task! It was at Dudley that I experienced the full range of tasks involved in operating a large branch store. The two 'vans' already mentioned were allied with petrol mobile butchers – Bedford as I remember. All of this and a far larger group of staff served the Dudley, Weetslade and part of Annitsford areas.

My first experience of driving came courtesy of a Smiths Electric and there was much more for a 'laddie' to occupy himself with here. Daily duties included, unlocking and taking in the heavy wooden gates covering the shop entrance, sweeping the area of pavement immediately outside of the front shop, sweeping floors front and back, unloading the lorry when the weekly order arrived from central stores each Thursday, assisting with other deliveries, running messages – well, you get the picture. The Danish bacon lorry would arrive fortnightly with our order of 'full sides', literally a pig cut in half length ways, a 'three quarter' which was a middle with either ham or shoulder still attached, a 'middle' being the part with the ribs that produces streaky bacon and usually a supply of extra hams and shoulders. The lorries were not refrigerated at this time and bacon was usually wrapped in hessian sacking and hung on racks. This of course proved to be a problem especially during the summer months. It was quite common to discover that the sides were fly blown and my first experience of this was quite shocking. Included in the duties that were incumbent upon me was instruction in boning and rolling and generally preparing bacon for sale on the provisions counter. On this particular day I began to 'bone' a side and found that flies had laid their eggs in the holes left by the hooks. The little wrigglers swarmed out as I removed the ribs it was like something from a horror movie or an 'x film' as it was at the time. The two sensations I remember were revulsion and then panic – what was to be done? Our old foreman told me to apply the time honoured method of disposing of unwelcome 'extra meat'. I was told to fill the big sink with water, mix in a full bag of salt, wash off the maggots and then continue as if nothing had been amiss. The bacon, after being neatly sliced and displayed on trays was destined for the provisions counter where I would often serve. Customers would comment on how fresh and lean the bacon looked. If they had seen it a half hour before their comments may have been a little different.

The provisions counter also displayed cut meats, butter, cheese etc. This was the sort of cheese with strength enough to bring tears to the eyes and a purse to the lips. Shoppers today buy cheese that has been moderated. Its strength and taste has been engineered to make it more appealing to the widest audience – 'dumbed' down I believe is the term. Cheese came in large 'rounds' wrapped in waxed cheese cloth for freshness, cut by hand, weighed and wrapped – with the same process applying to butter. Before pre weighing and wrapping, butter came to us in wooden barrels – one barrel shaped, four stone block of finest Danish butter. This had to be cut into weights of a quarter, half and pound blocks then wrapped in greaseproof paper and stored in the cooling counter – in those days margarine was generally only used in cooking.

Some local Dudley children gather outside the Inn, being curious of the postcard photographer. Perhaps I served them as adults over 50 years later.

Bacon was cut on an old Berkel machine made of solid steel and incredibly heavy. The roll of bacon was clamped to the flat bed ready for cutting. The operator would set the thickness of slices on the blade, usually number 4 for bacon, the wheel was turned by hand and the cutting could begin. The bed slid back and forth and after each slice moved close to the blade to allow the next slice to be cut. The blade itself was circular almost two feet across and was wickedly sharp. Tales abounded throughout the branches of operators who had lost fingers and even hands. It was fearsome machine that I had to clean and sharpen each night. An old chap from Berkels arrived periodically to service the beast. He could strip it down with the ease that familiarity brings. I could not watch as he handled the razor sharp blade as though it was no more dangerous than a frisbee!

I also got the opportunity to learn something of the butchering business while at Dudley. In intimate knowledge of the anatomy of the beast is gained while being the agent of its final destruction. At the rear of the butchers shop was a small outhouse used for storing bones. Once every week or so, a large open backed lorry would call to collect the bones for delivery to glue makers and to be ground down for agricultural use. During the summer months the lorry seemed to be permanently attended by a swarm of fat black flies. We always knew when it had arrived for the smell even indoors was nauseating. My old gran used to say that there was usually a benefit to be found in any bad situation if it was looked for hard enough. It was the anglers of Dudley who reaped the harvest of this particular silver lining. The outhouse where the bones were stored became a teaming nursery for flies with maggots available by the bucketful. One local angler was heard to say to his wife 'I'm just off to the butchers for some maggots pet.'

The tradition of providing doorstep sales to local communities had been followed by the society almost from its inception. I well remember the 'Store' greengrocer, his cart piled with a colourful display of fruit and vegetables and the baker with freshly baked bread in large wicker trays. Both would be pulled by beautiful big horses chosen for their placid nature.

The carts were always well turned out, painted green with red and gold lettering. Horses were always immaculately groomed with harness leather and brass shining. The larger of the two mobile shops was driven by a local lady. She was known in the village and to everyone on her round as a jovial, loud, kind lady who was particularly well placed to harvest the local gossip. I was given to her to 'train up' in the ways of 'the van'. The smallest van was manned by a friendly, nervous little chap

A procession of Co-op carts and horses.

who was a bit over fond of the drink. As well as groceries our vans carried large barrels of sherry. Customers would bring their own bottles which would be filled from the barrel for a few shillings. He would often return from his round with a waver in his walk, a silly grin and smelling for all the world like he had been drinking but swearing otherwise. I remember a butcher working from Cramlington central being inordinately fond of the 'Highland Dew'. He would receive his 'glass' from many of his customers during the Christmas and New Year period. There were a number of incidents over the years in which he and his mobile butchery had to be retrieved from somewhere in Cramlington as he had been found drunk behind the counter. I seem to be wandering from the point.

To most of our customers on the round our regular weekly appearance was a pleasant convenience. To some however, it was not only this but also an important connection to the outside world. It was my task when we reached the Aged Miners Cottages in Dudley or Weetslade or Annitsford to alert the old folk that we have arrived. Those that could walk, I would help on to the van; others I would take their lists of groceries and get the items for them. The accounts of tea we drank at these stops became dangerous as toilets were in short supply!

The 'round' took us on a different route each day. We always tried to finish before the shop closed for the day but this was not always possible. Our stops had to be completed no matter how long it took and many times especially on Fridays this could be nine in the evening. On Saturday mornings, the round would take us to the outlying houses and the cottages at the south of Dudley. Half day closing on Saturday, we were always finished on time. It was at some point during all of this that I was allowed to drive our 'van' for the first time. The Smiths mobile shop had two rows of single cell batteries, one each side of the vehicle and located under the floor. They had to be charged every night and kept topped up with distilled water. It was the width of the thing that made for tricky driving for novices. Three clicks of the pedal would get about twenty mph out of it but this was increased to thirty by hitting the booster button on the steering column. After finishing the round early one day I was taken for a driving lesson on to the back roads at Arcot Hall. Anyone who knows the area will know that the stretch of road between Dam Dykes and Beacon Hill is particularly narrow, and fringed by quite deep ditches in certain stretches. It was on one of those stretches that the edge of the road gave way and our pride and

An advert for the Cramlington District Co-operative Society Ltd.

joy clattered into the ditch. Everything flew off the shelves, all was chaos and embarrassment was great. Dam Dykes Farm provided the phone and, within one hour, two guys from the Central Workshops arrived in a Willys Jeep to tow us out of the ditch. Our manager at the time was not feted for his good humour and tolerance of an underlining such as myself. However, after a plausible explanation I seemed to have got away with only black looks and the silent treatment for a few days.

I have a claim to fame regarding my travelling shop days. One of my customers was Mrs Green who would bring her son Robson to the van each Saturday morning. Robson Green of course, known for all manner of TV roles, singing and exploits with big fish.

In those days of course, most of the collieries in the area were still open and working so our branch did a brisk trade in chewing tobacco. Uncle Jeff Pigtail would often be bought by the good wives of Dudley with their weekly shop. At first I found this a little puzzling, not being able to work out why women would want a six inch twist of solid tobacco. Although at least one old lady in the village still smoked a clay pipe. It was explained to me that the 'twist' was bought for a husband miner who would chew the stuff while working underground. Smoking at the 'face' or anywhere within the mine was strictly forbidden for obvious reasons so miners who smoked would chew tobacco instead. I tried it once but no one told me not to swallow the juice. I did, and it was a bad idea.

I remember great excitement in the village with the arrival of a BBC film unit in Burradon, just a short distance from Dudley. The BBC were dramatising Zola's Classic *Germinal*. As Dudley Colliery was a relatively recent endeavour, they chose Burradon to shoot the scenes required. Burradon was far older and its buildings and ambience more fitting to the classic story. Anyway, when the hungry crew and cast had cleaned out the shops in Burradon, including the Society's branch shop, they descended upon Dudley. In so doing we were informed that extras were required to appear in some scenes. Applicants must be small, under-nourished, gaunt, hollow eyed and be prepared to wear rags and walk with a shuffle. Our foreman, who was an ex desert rat and could take me to a large stock of 'bully beef' he had buried in the Libyan desert, was perfect for the part of a down-trodden half starved French miner. He even had a 'graveyard' cough brought about by forty Capstan full strength a day.

I left Dudley and the Society after three enjoyable years. I almost forgot I got all this fun and was paid six pounds a week, less off takes!

Dudley Colliery, around 1910.

Cramlington District Co-operative Society Chemistry Drug Department.

Co-op Square in the 1970s, showing the old Post Office building (right) which later become the Co-op Chemist. The shop on the end of the row is the Co-operative Society's original chemist shop (*shown on the photograph at the top of the page*). The beautiful Edwardian frontage having been painted over to present a particularly unappealing aspect. The shop was later used as the hardware department of Cramlington Co-op.

Above: The Co-op Central Premises, Cramlington. The store was divided into departments and on the left are the 'Drapery' and 'Millinery' Departments.

Left: The Cramlington Co-op Central Buildings in the 1970s.

Left: The demolition of Cramlington Co-op Central Buildings in the 1970s.

War and Peace

Two Cramlington men who served.

Left: A photograph by Cuttriss of Newcastle of Harry Dormand of Cramlington, Northumberland Fusiliers. Dormand is an old Cramlington name and no doubt Harry's descendants are still thriving.

Far left: Joe Hall, complete with swagger stick, Royal Artillery, circa 1916.

Left: Two examples of cards produced by good old R. Johnston & Son, Gateshead for the military training camps in the Cramlington area. The lower card says: 'Greetings from the Brigade Camp 'Somewhere'. Keep it dark'.

'Somewhere' is also probably Horton Camp. The small circular photograph on the left of the Horton card matches the top left hand image on the lower card.

Summer 1919 and the Cramlington 'Peace Arch' is one of many thousands across the country, erected to celebrate the end of the 'Great war for civilisation'.

A Victory Bonfire ready to be lit to celebrate the end of the First World War.

A card by Johnston of Gateshead showing the War Memorial which was unveiled with much ceremony in 1922.

The unveiling of Cramlington Village War Memorial in 1922. My father remembered attending the ceremony with my grandfather Harry Godfrey. He said that the crush was so great that they could not get closer than the chapel. The photograph shows the wooden platform set up for dignitaries as well as the public; military personnel including nurses are also present. The building around the square has changed little since this photograph was taken and the memorial, with its immortal names, is still venerated by many.

The First World War was said to be the 'war to end all wars' however, twenty years later once again the world was engulfed in conflict. Here is an image from Second World War showing a march past of Home Guardsmen at High Pit in 1942. The men are probably from 17th Northumberland (Ashington) Battalion.

Glimpses of old Cramlington

An aerial view of Cramlington Village in 1923. Little would have changed in the village since 1915 where Kapitan-Leutnant Mathy of Zeppelin L9 would have had a similar view. Cramlington Hall can be seen nestled in the trees at the right of the photograph. At bottom, middle is Thompson Brothers market garden, which once belonged to the hall grounds and is now the site of Manor Walks and the new cinema complex. The Co-op buildings are at left and are long gone. The rows of low buildings next to the open space are pig sties. Pigs were reared here and slaughter day was on a Thursday. Taking a short cut while returning from school I remember blood on the cobbles and unearthly squeals coming from the building with two arches at extreme left. The heart of the village is little changed. A lot of buildings of East Middle and West Farms have been retained, re-vamped and reused. West Farm is at extreme left, just below the Council Schools building with the 'L' shaped row of buildings being 'Laurel Cottages' now 'Laurel Place'. Just across the road from here is the 'Travellers Rest' and 'Low Main Place' where the L9's incendiary bomb exploded in Bell's Yard. The open fields at the top of the photograph are now largely covered by modern housing estates.

Cramlington Village

Left: Cramlington Village – an Auty of Tynemouth card.

40

Cramlington Railway Station dated from the mid 19th century. The Victorian cast iron footbridge can be seen with the 'new' road bridge in the background. The buildings from the top are the engine shed, booking office and waiting room and a row of houses for station employees. It can be presumed that living so close to the main Newcastle to Edinburgh line would pose noise problems. I am

assured by others who live just as close in Nelson Village that the train noise quickly becomes commonplace and virtually unnoticeable.

Cramlington Station Terrace and Stanley Houses in the 1970s. Apart from the houses in the middle distance all of the buildings in this photograph have gone. The view was taken from the Victorian cast iron footbridge in the station and shows Station Terrace at right with Stanley houses at left. To the left of the house with the arched doorway is a low wall about five feet long. This is the only survivor in this photograph – beneath the turf today lays a flight of stone stairs that lead to the arched doorway.

Osbourne Terrace in the 1960s with the station buildings in the background.

A 19th century view of the West Cramlington Pit. Four girls pose in the foreground on the railway line while a pitman and pony are in the background.

The Annie Pit, East Cramlington. The pit was closed in 1938 and is now the site of the TA Building.

The Lamb Pit, East Cramlington that was demolished in 1960.

Cramlington Welfare FC in the mid 1930s. Back row: C. Nesbitt, W. Dishman, J. Davison (Capt), T. Malone, W. Wright, S. Johnson, T. Worth (Trainer). Front row: T. Reilly, W. Spry, J. Henderson, J. Herron, L. Bell. Previously known as Cramlington Rovers, they became members of Cramlington and District League. This is one of dozens of North East football teams featured on Ardath Tobacco cigarette cards – another featured side was East Cramlington Black Watch FC.

The lone survivor of a row of 18th century cottages became Cramlington's blacksmiths shop. The 'Smith' would have been quite busy chap in horse drawn days making horseshoes, shoeing, making farm implements etc. I remember the smith at work amid a gloomy shop. Its walls hung with tools, the air heavy with smoke and ringing metal and its molten heat glowing white. The building was demolished in 1974 but the area retains the name of 'Smithy Square'. The building in the background is the house of the Thompson Brothers. Thompson's Market Garden served Cramlington for many years with their home grown vegetables and fruit. The shop was located in the original house, decrepit and used only for storage and selling produce to the public. After the house was demolished the front garden and its paths were left for a number of years as a pleasant mini park. The contraption in the photograph below is interesting and essential as it saved a massive amount of hard work. The soil within the greenhouses would have to be changed after two growing seasons but for this engine. Not being subjected to normal weather conditions soil is allowed to harbour disease and all manner of nasty things that plants are not happy with. A full head of steam on the engine was required. The steam was fed under pressure through pipes into the green houses and blasted through the soil, killing everything. The soil would recover naturally helped by quantities of farmyard manure.

Left and above: Four photographs of West Farm outbuildings before demolition. The building in the photograph above is typical of Northumbrian farms. At ground level are the byres, in which cattle could be over wintered. Above the byres was one long space suitable for storage, hay, straw, cattle feed etc. At the West end of this building was a raised wooden platform about two feet high and four feet wide across the whole width of the floor. This had obviously been a stage used for theatrical performances as the wall behind had been plastered and bore traces of painted decoration. The walls around the stage area bore the remains of gas mantles – the whole place could have seated thirty or forty people comfortably. Access to the upper floor was through a door at the rear which led directly onto a wooden staircase. It is easy to imagine the sound of the British Army boots tramping up these stairs to attend a company entertainment or perhaps a temperance meeting with the audience being quite sparse, I fancy.

Above: Believe it or not, this is now the lounge of the Plough pub in Cramlington Village. Gale force winds at Christmas 1975 stripped the remaining tiles from the roof of the gin gan at Middle Farm. The two trees to the right are growing in the school playing field and are still doing fine.

Above: This is a school photograph possibly taken at Cramlington Old School, circa 1890s. The school was built in 1853 by Mr Shaun Storey of Arcot Hall. It later became the Parish Hall and then retail premises.

Right: The Old School building as it looked after a devastating fire in the 1970s. The Travellers rest can be seen with West farm builds in the distance.

Left: Station Terrace under demolition. The site is now occupied by Cramlington Retail Park.

Cramlington Council Schools. In 2013 it is boarded up and awaiting demolition. When I was a pupil at this school, during winter months when snow lay on the schoolyard, the diamond stone set into the chimney stack was a target for snowballs – great prestige could be gained from a successful throw.

A postcard of the Miners' Homes, around 1920. Another card from Robert Johnston.

The Wesleyan Chapel. The old chapel had had many incarnations since last used as a place of worship. I remember attending Sunday school here. As well as being used by a glazing firm, the chapel's last occupant was an Italian restaurant. The building is now not in use – the last venture having failed – and awaits its next re-birth.

Robert and Norman Foster with their charabanc on an outing somewhere in Northumberland 1923. Fosters Garage and yard was situated at the station end of Station Terrace. They did haulage repairs.

Splendidly attired in shiny black top hat and red coat, Arnold Foster sits atop of what would have been a familiar mode of transport in 1924.

Left: A Cramlington Village School photograph from around 1923-25. In the back row, fourth left, is John George Raffle. His brother Gordon is in the second row from the front, third left. Sadly Gordon was killed at Dunkirk during the Second World War.

This is another photograph that could have been taken in the 1950s. Socks that refused to stay up and 'gansies' knitted by your granny were still standard issue for boys when I was at school!

Another Cramlington Village School photograph from around 1923-25. Standing in the centre of the third row from the front, wearing a white pinafore, is my mother Beattie Godfrey (née Collier). The teacher on the right is Mr Hubbard who she remembers as being a 'nice man'. Mother remains hale and hearty, still playing piano at ninety-years-old. The little girl, second row, on the right, looks to be well chewed off with the whole business!